John Lewis
Congressman & Civil Rights Activist

by Grace Hansen

Abdo
HISTORY MAKER
BIOGRAPHIES
Kids

abdobooks.com

Published by Abdo Kids, a division of ABDO, P.O. Box 398166, Minneapolis, Minnesota 55439.
Copyright © 2022 by Abdo Consulting Group, Inc. International copyrights reserved in all countries.
No part of this book may be reproduced in any form without written permission from the publisher.
Abdo Kids Jumbo™ is a trademark and logo of Abdo Kids.

Printed in the United States of America, North Mankato, Minnesota.

052021

092021

THIS BOOK CONTAINS
RECYCLED MATERIALS

Photo Credits: Alamy, Getty Images, iStock, Shutterstock PREMIER, ©Kreeder13 p.5 / CC BY-SA 4.0

Production Contributors: Teddy Borth, Jennie Forsberg, Grace Hansen
Design Contributors: Candice Keimig, Pakou Moua

Library of Congress Control Number: 2021932504
Publisher's Cataloging-in-Publication Data

Names: Hansen, Grace, author.

Title: John Lewis: congressman & civil rights activist / by Grace Hansen

Other title: congressman & civil rights activist

Description: Minneapolis, Minnesota : Abdo Kids, 2022 | Series: History maker biographies | Includes
    online resources and index.

Identifiers: ISBN 9781098208912 (lib. bdg.) | ISBN 9781098209056 (ebook) | ISBN 9781098209124
    (Read-to-Me ebook)

Subjects: LCSH: Lewis, John, 1940-2020--Juvenile literature. | Legislators--United States--Biography--
    Juvenile literature. | Civil rights workers--Biography--Juvenile literature. | African American political
    activists--Biography--Juvenile literature.

Classification: DDC 328.73092--dc23

Table of Contents

Early Life & Education

John Lewis was born on February 21, 1940, near Troy, Alabama. His parents, Eddie and Mae, were **sharecroppers**. After many years, they eventually had their own land to farm.

Alabama

John spent his early years **segregated** in school and public life. John knew segregation was wrong. His parents asked him not to talk about it with others. They didn't want him to get in trouble or hurt.

WAITING ROOM
FOR WHITE ONLY
←
BY ORDER
POLICE DEPT.

7

Civil Rights Leader

Lewis was the first person in his family to attend college. He went to Fisk University, in Nashville, Tennessee. He earned a degree in Religion and **Philosophy**.

9

In college, he learned about peaceful protests. Lewis was a natural leader. This helped him plan and participate in **sit-ins** and **Freedom Rides**.

These events protested **segregation** laws. And just as his parents thought, Lewis was hurt by people who did not agree with him. But Lewis never became violent himself.

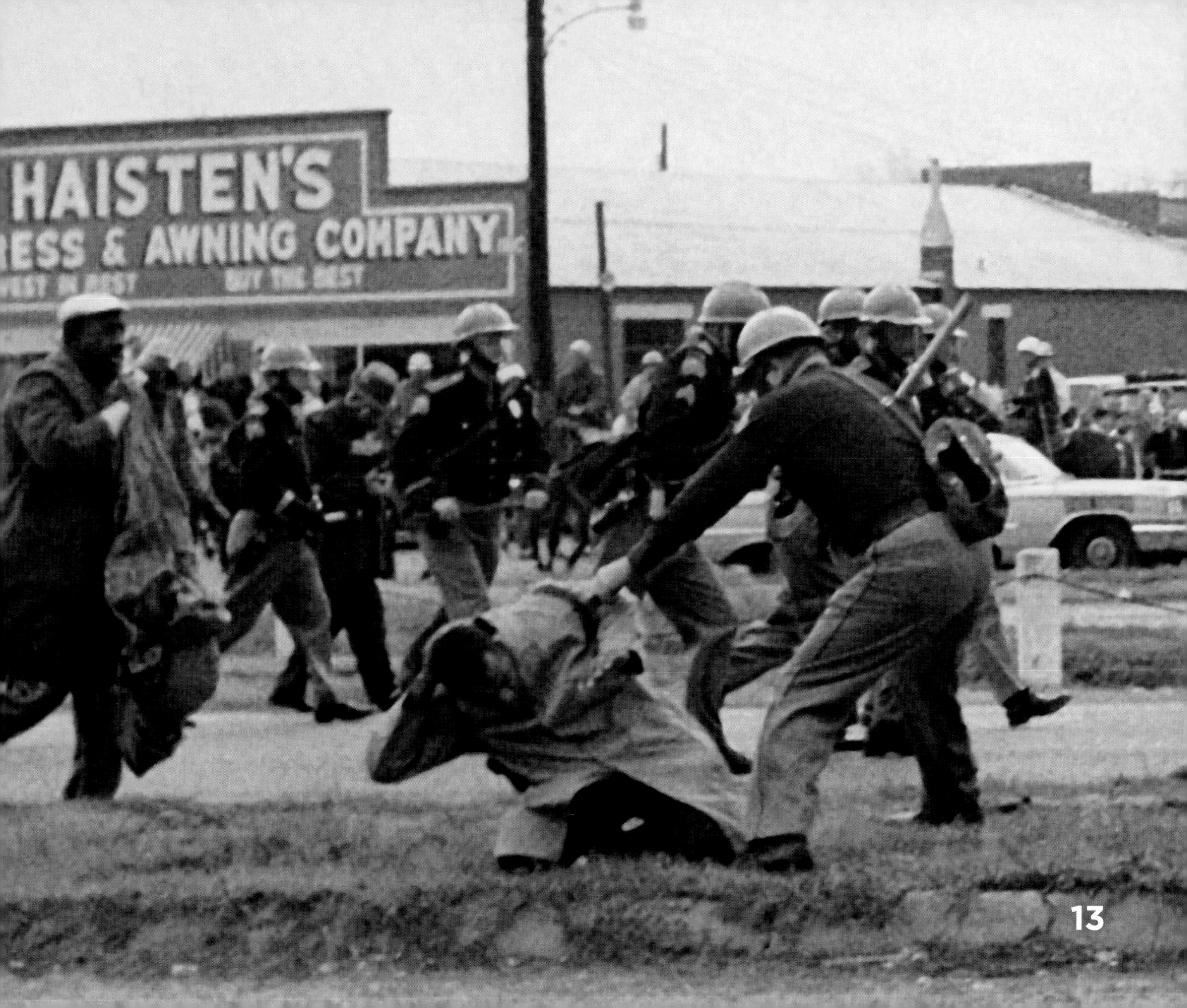
HAISTEN'S
RESS & AWNING COMPANY
BUY THE BEST

In August of 1963, Lewis spoke at the March on Washington. He also helped plan the historic event. He was just 23 years old.

In 1977, President Jimmy Carter asked Lewis to head an agency called ACTION. It helped manage people in the Peace Corps. Then in 1981, Lewis ran for and won a seat on the Atlanta City Council.

US Congressman

In 1986, Lewis again set his sights on the nation's capital. He wanted to make change from the inside. He ran for **Congress** and won. He served in the House for more than 30 years.

19

Death & Legacy

John Lewis died of cancer on July 17, 2020. Lewis dedicated his life to fighting for civil rights and equality. He is remembered for inspiring change and a better tomorrow.

Timeline

March 7
Lewis and thousands of others protest voting rights in Selma, Alabama. Lewis is badly injured by police in a day remembered as Bloody Sunday.

November 4
Lewis is elected to Congress. In his career, he is re-elected 16 times to represent Georgia's 5th District.

July 17
Lewis passes away at the age of 80.

1965

1986

2020

1940

1959

1963

1981

2011

February 21
John Lewis is born near Troy, Alabama.

Lewis
participates in workshops on peaceful protesting.

August 28
Lewis speaks at the March on Washington, a historic event he helped plan.

October 6
Lewis is elected to the Atlanta City Council.

Lewis is awarded the Presidential Medal of Freedom.

Glossary

Congress – the branch of the US government that is elected to make laws. Congress is made up of the Senate and the House of Representatives.

Freedom Ride – any of the bus trips taken by civil rights activists in the 1960s which served to highlight and challenge racial discrimination in the US.

philosophy – the study of the nature of life, truth, knowledge, and other important human matters.

segregation – to unfairly separate people according to groups, especially racial groups. The process of segregating is segregation.

sharecropper – a tenant farmer who gives a portion of his or her crop to the owner of the land as rent.

sit-in – an act of occupying seats in a segregated establishment in organized protest against discrimination.

Index

Abdo Kids
ONLINE
FREE! ONLINE MULTIMEDIA RESOURCES

Visit **abdokids.com** to access crafts, games, videos, and more!

Use Abdo Kids code

HJK8912

or scan this QR code!